CLUTCH PLATES

CLUTCH PLATES

Poems

By

WILLIAM PAGE

Boston
BRANDEN PRESS
Publishers

ACKNOWLEDGMENTS

Some of these poems first appeared in the following publications: *Antigonish Review, Descant, Epos, The Falcon, Manroot, Mississippi Review, Pembroke Magazine, Poem, River City Review, Road Apple Review, South Carolina Review, Southern Poetry Review, Sou'wester Literary Quarterly,* and *Wisconsin Review.* Some of these poems are forthcoming in an anthology under the editorship of Kirby Congdon.

The front cover photograph, courtesy of Hi-Torque Publications, is reproduced from *Choppers Magazine,* May, 1968, copyright by Ed Roth.

For Nancy

CONTENTS

THE GLIDING

BONES FROM THE EARTH

TOUCHING THE PAST

THE THIRST

CLUTCH PLATES

THE GLIDING

Parts

Only a magnesium spoke holding together
a road.
Just a linked chain
pulling teeth out of a river.

Motorcycle gloves listening
to the black drip
of oil, a hissing in the gear box.

And a rearview
mirror
forgetting its eyes.

Over in the corner
a stack of bent frames coughing.
And where is the pin

that threatened to leave,
where is the saddle
remembering a rider?

Mojave Night

Heat comes flowing up,
                    to this
cold night—and takes
   me back to hot Mojave.

Up ahead one red light,
another bike I might
outrun if I turn it on.

But road's a shifting
sand.
            Beware of speed,
                4 A.M. 105 degrees.
Hearing's a forgotten line
the miles and altitude have
memorized.
                The coyote swims
in the lambent beam,
   disappearing into itself.

Needles strike my face, hard,
and all my ambivalent arms
        smell of leather.

   The engine bloods
      my leg, a cold fire.

The hand curls
   a withered leaf.

   Along the roadside
      are abandoned cars—

The Motorcycle
as an Instrument of Delusion

Stars hanging
from your feet.
Motorcycle, Mother. You've
got to own one to
put the ground beneath
you. Ride thru

the arch of death.
To know your glass
brow, the color
of your shit, the lip

of sunshine.
Ride, Mother. To
hear the diamond
on the rattler, to

spend your arms
across the night.
Look thru the
window of the sun.

Sing the throat
of moons,
of hands
falling into shadows.
Ride, Mother,
around the rings of trees,
thru the kiss
of anger, the bloody tits
of rage. Motorcycle,
Mother. Ride

till you begin to feel
the balls of fire
slipping
from your eyes.

Lament for a Dead Motorcyclist

Tricycle wheels spin
thru every kid's head.
Even your dreams
must have clanked
like a drive chain.

By thirty-two, why should
we have expected more
than to see you throbbing
thru a pair of cylinders
stinking with death?

You wondered what made me
jealous of a piece of iron,
when your cock didn't stay
where it belonged
half the time, or why

I cried when you left
each time, but didn't
when you came limping
back with broken scars.

You put on your swastikaed costume,
ranting about your freedom.
I never understood how fierce independence
squared with a club demanding uniforms.

Surely even an oily-
haired bike jockey like you
understood a basic law of physics:

If you run into the side
of a truck at sixty,

you don't ride back.

Why did you have to
lean on a spoked
wheel, rusting like
a broken star?

Couldn't you
grow up
out of your iron myth?

The Gliding

Look into the rearview mirror
    even look back
    & nobody's there,
and then   half way   into the lane
    there it comes.   I'm gliding
        towards it.
    My God it's really there, blue
    & big   & out of ...
Later he'll say, "God Man, I'm sorry.
    I guess I was going
too fast.   You really hurt?"
    Now I'm just thinking of that
    blue car in the way of a "Bike"
        I can't turn fast enough.

    Just a blam of my wheel
up against that blue sedan.
Then the slam hard asphalt—
    sliding along on it,
still in the saddle
    & my foot hung up
    in the frame,
    and I don't even
    know it,
        just know
I'm going down on the clearest
    day in October
    sliding along
on my side & a red "Bike,"
leaving cloth, paint, sparks
    & skin on the asphalt.
    Glass cracking out of the single
    headlight.
& that's it.

Then
   hobbling to the bleeding curb,
         my ankle
               torn to the bone.

Disappointing the intern
   (in the emergency room)
   who hoped the bone was
               broken.
"Sometimes a broken bone
         absorbs the shock, causing
less severe damage to the vascular system."

Later, the surgeon cuts a slab off your thigh
         & sews it on down there
               like patching a hole in
               a quilt/ except there isn't any quilt
         but a green sheet
               between your eyes
         & your wound & you feel
               the punch-cutting/ the stitching-pressure
         & sweat till he's finished &
               you walk with a cane
                  out of the operating room.

And if the graft
   doesn't take, well,
               what the hell?
      Harleys shift on the left
         side anyway.
   And we all go down on a clear
         day in October.

BONES FROM THE EARTH

A Touch of Elegance

The elevator
bows obsequiously,
slowly hums its descent
like a fading doxology.

Inside, my father
lies in a soft blue bag
like the velvet gloves
silver goblets
are stored in.

The Bird on the Limb

He'll want to go down to the "Yeller Dog."
        They cry every day
if you let them; wet for attention.

In a dentist's chair my mouth is hot
        with wax; the doctor pokes
his finger at my jaw, explaining to Dad
        something about a chin I don't
understand. And Mother is home washing
        my jeans, forgiving the pen.

The stooped lady wanders the halls
        squeezing hands for "them." And Uncle
Charlie in his wheel chair is singing with-
        out teeth to the gentle "women-ladies,"
thankful for his food and two hands to eat it.

In the cloakroom Tommy is shooting dice
        when snake-eyes look up and bite him.
The nickel Indians lie with their ears to
        the floor, listening. And Lincoln fades
in our dreams of riches no one has seen. We
        line up in rows when the fire bell rings.

Outside a single bird is frozen on the limb.
        Dad sends me to the fountain with a glass
in my hand; he clutches in his fist a rainbow.
        Old Savage drives his mules, gee and hawing
until they respond. "All crazy or get that way,"
        the nurse whispers who bathes him.

The boney man with a wen like a knapsack says,
        "Good Morning." I'm somewhere with
an out-of-tune piano and don't hear him, or

putting my books on a table. And so
I take my plate with a shiny fork in the center
and wait my turn in the kitchen.

The Man with the Silver Holder

The Cadillac stands
in the drive.
The stickpin
is the flicked tongue
in the tie. Knotted
like a snake it glitters
in the dawn. The diamond ring,
big as a barn, flashes
on his hand. With it
he could scratch his name
on the little town.
Like a patrician he beckons
the mercy of time. He grows
the rose whose thorns
comb the wind, as he bends
to the care of the leaf.

Here is the silver holder
clenched in his teeth
like the dream of a storm,
here is the smile on his
palm he leaves behind
when he rises.
And last but not least
is the hand he raises
to shade his face
from the sun.

Thistle

The cigarette ash
falls. It is
the sky. The thistle
blooms lavender, the goldfinch
flies under the porch roof.
My father is shining
his car, sleeves muscled-up
against his arms.
At a quarter till four
on a Sunday afternoon
we will drive by the park.
The thick hairs of his forearm
are blown by the wind.
The cold orange sun
sits in the window.
At home the scream
of a band saw
will call our attention
until nightfall.
He will tell me
a tale of dipping his cup
into the frozen milk.
I dream of learning to skate
in the basement, falling
thru the floor, thru
the rocks and dirt
to awake with the workbench
spinning in my head.
Father is gripping
a wheel at ten and four,
shoulders wide,
foot pressed
to the floor, he glides
silently thru town

past the farms,
the cities
and won't stop
again for anyone.

Bones from the Earth

You sit in my head rocking
compressed like a photograph
in a little chair.
The gray hair hangs
around your neck
like sea foam.

This too will pass.

You have come to tell me
the lightning does not burn
the rain,
the roots of the maple stick
like bones from the brown earth.

You held me in hands of feathers.

Each morning I am like dew
on an ancient grave.
My spine is a sleeping tree
prophetic as a golden mask.
The field is laced with sparrows.

Now you are gnawing, now erupting
like the bowels of a pig.

The fur grows thick on the beaver
and the gray morning rolls in
like a ball.

The first crossing is by fire,
the second by water, you tell me.
You who have come back
kneeling beside the black cat,

thru layers of earth and years,
digging like a blind beast,
you have shoveled open
your grave and I must
bury you again.

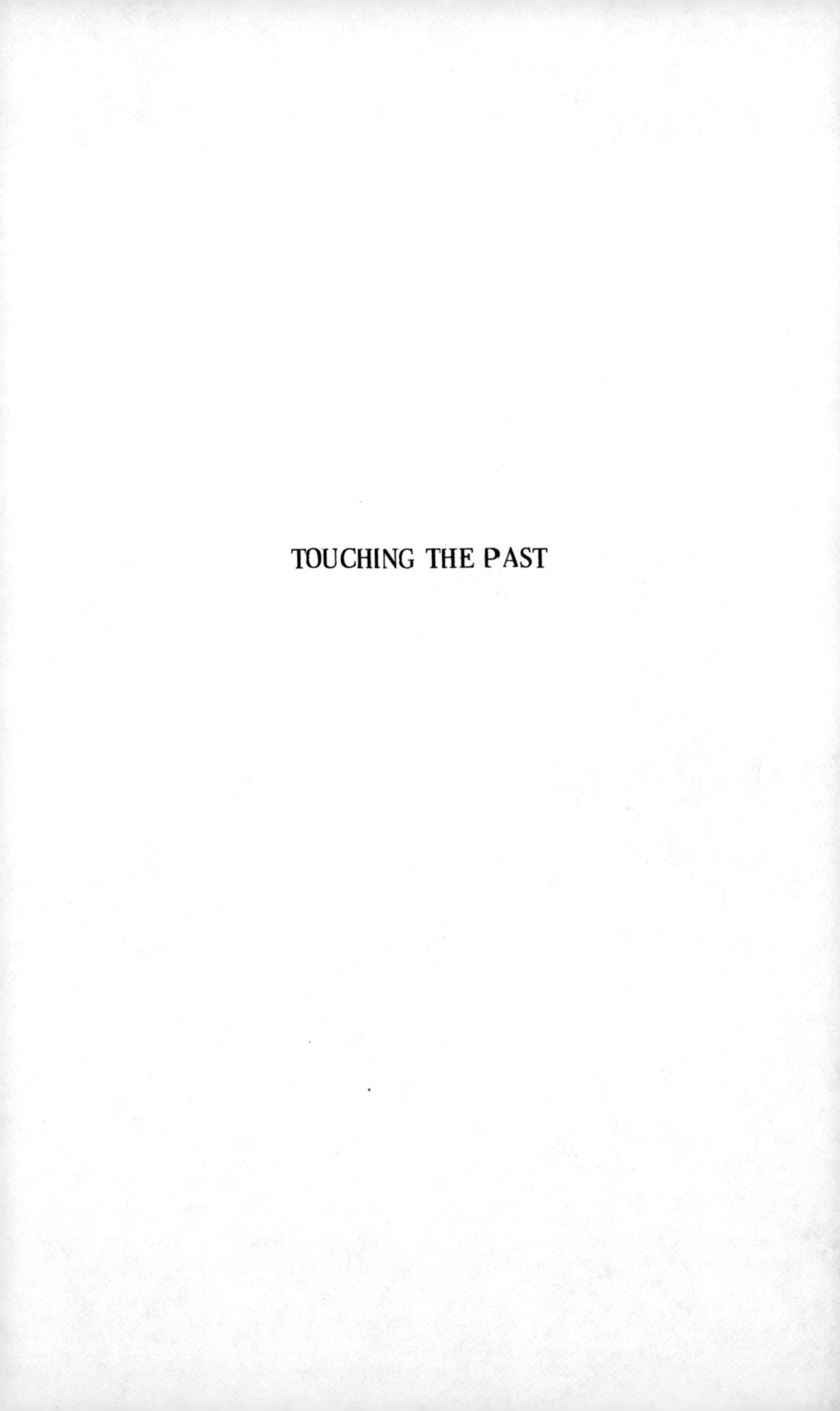

TOUCHING THE PAST

Plates

And the cigarette wound
in my shirt like a wen.

And I am driving back
to the dump trucks,

bulldogs growling,

the amber lights floating
in an empty shell.

My foot shoves thru the firewall.

Valve chatter down the rat
holes, the carburetor

sucking the nipple,
the fan belt weary and screaming.
The pure cylinders churn into milk pails,
buckshot in the sign of curves.

Clutch plates like a nest of eggs,
and the drive shaft oiled and shining

rides like a moon,
a hunger for the road. Dignity

in a bruised hand, love
in a leather apron. A broken pump,

and day breaks on the hood.

Aubade 1940

An iron bed sweats
in the dormers.

What can I find
scratching the itch
of insulation
between the joists
or straightening nails,
hammering the half-moons
into the 2×4's?

The naked bulb hangs down,
the night's cold filament
an icicle of sleep.

A bell goes off
in the kitchen.
From the burnt toast
the knife scrapes
the black snow.

Thru the triangular
hole, I pour the morning.
While yesterday's faces
lie by the butter,
a silent dog
whimpers at the door.

Green La Salle

When we were eighteen
everybody still called you "Ace."
The heaviest thing about you
was your red hair.
You were the kind of kid
who pulled the sheet back
to see if there was breathing.

Back there in the chest of hills
you still snickered
behind Betsy's teeth.
My dad's green La Salle
starts its motor every time
I hear the crack of pool balls.

That long drive we made
one week-end when
I looked out the window
to see the forest walking
into the cold wind, that
was the last time
I saw you without
the wrinkles of experience.

How many sharp turns
have you drunk since then?
How many friends
have you passed
as the windshield
falls on your face
this morning?

Feeding the Dogs

We take the seat
from the back
for the haul.
Burlap replaces their straw.

Where the windows
sing to the doves.

The pan of cornbread
simmers by the stand.
The cats eat table scraps
we thank the Lord.

After we sold Joe
he trotted home
thru the roads and briars.

The raw bone
of the forest whistles.
The guns are cold
in our hands.

Mother has lit the oven.
Cracked the egg
in the battered pan.

Joe used to flail
his tail like a whip
till it almost hurt
my leg.

Then there was Mac
with his nervous hair
breathing the cloud of fog.
He rattles the pan
with his nose.

Rack

Johnny, your gentleness
grew like a green field
against a brown pony.
A ball of sun shone
in your chalk eyes.
Between your flecked teeth
you bit off a toothpick,
or from your lips the smoke
dangled and flipped.
Your hands were as hard
as ball cracking tables,
but the voice thin
as the beaded wire
counting our score.
In the back room, where
the faces of cards growled
and smoke hung,
I saw you serve up
the foaming beer
running down the edge
of mugs.
From a pure glass jar
the zinc went howling down
your throat, the cue
banged against the oily floor,
the stale cough clamored
into echoes,
and then the call for "rack"!
And with the triangle
on your arm, you were gone.

Pockets

Father's broad brimmed hat—
Father in the box of
lost stuff. Which closet
did we keep it in? The
box of lost change, one
glove, two pens, a sweater.
Are you still shifting thru
the blue muffler, half a pair
of size ten overshoes, a torn
raincoat, a two dollar bill,
a broken umbrella and
a roll of unexposed film?
How far back can I see
thru the cracked sunglasses?

If I take home the torn
raincoat, no one will know.
When I reach down
this time I see polka dots
on the back of my hand.
The movie doors are shut,
the seats sold to the circus
long ago. Only the cold
concrete floor remains.
But I'm trying to reach down
with my cupped breath.
The wrist watch, still moving,
shows a loss of time.
The second hand is twirling
too late for you.

Somewhere, old man, you put
on a coat with two
buttons missing, as if

you didn't leave everything behind.
I pull the tight skull cap
down over my head
like a first aviator.
And in the depths of my hand
I look for a lost key.
I slip on the one lost
glove, feeling the fur
you no longer need.

From the dark casket of old clothes
I pull my hand back.
The veins in the
back of my hand stand out
like smoke from chimneys.
Another lost item
among the rubble of
Sunday matinees.
I try to read the objects
left behind. I puzzle
over the carved characters in
the chair arms among the sticky
smell of memories.

The clothes tear away,
old man, bursting
the seams of your face.
I try to sew up the holes
in the pockets of the past
to keep from losing all.
Before the silence
tumbles out of boxes of lost clothes.

Reading Detective Magazines at the Home
of a Car Thief

The print blurs
in old magazines.
   Sandusky, Ohio clicks
like bullets ...

In a glass table the face
   of his sister appears.
   If she entices me,
      I won't resist.

 We are inside the house
   circled by a frame of spraying
gravel,
         the smoke blooms inside
      like a gray flower, like
         a cancer hiding in the cupboard.

   There is the smell of crime
in the curtains,
      and under the window
   next to the body
         that resembles yours,
there is something missing.

Touching the Past

Hills stream down.
A night bus speeding
toward Oklahoma.
And I am reading
in the light
of a pencil.

The concrete bridges
settling down,
the houses burning behind
their windows.
The green plants rubbing
their hands.

Overhead the night of
Kansas says nothing.
I listen anyway.

Apples breathe
in the orchards
like dying vagrants.
Mothers everywhere stand
in shawls. The moon
limping into the kitchen.

Now the leaves are eating my house.
Children running snowless.
Jumping fences
no one has built.

The quail with their
enameled beaks
close their soft eyes

in a ring at my waist,
silent like the
hair of dogs.
The gun still warm
in its throat.

Wading through coffee
black as a morning face
my mother calls me.

From the weedy lot
where I am holding my death
in a glove, I see
my white hand like a butterfly
touching the black glass.
And I am saved.

THE THIRST

The Family

Our cave holds us
like the ribs
of a cage

and we are lonely
but do not know
it, cannot speak.

Thunderclouds outside
our dim lit home
frighten the nursing child.

We wait for the hunter
king's return
with meat and wounds.

Only the dropping
water strikes an art
in our shaggy brain.

The Thirst

(For Jim Dickey)

I followed you
to the inn
in the dark
striking my head
against the music
of the tavern.

At the band's last beat
my heart jumped
from my chest
like a sleeping fish.
I gripped my drink
hard as life.

We tried to talk
our mouths
opening fish-like,
chewing the air for words.

How much the twisted words
seem to tie us
in a knot like death.
When we seem to be drowning
in silence
perhaps we're only trying
to swim back to a distant bank
remembered in a dream.

We drain our glasses,
hoping for the right word,
the living gesture
when the long night

puts his arm around us
like a friendly drunk
and vomits us up
into the reeling blackness.

The Red Dress

(Anne Sexton, d. 1974)

Readers in libraries
always look lonely
as if they'd just given away

a gold watch
they hadn't wound
for years.

In their eyes
is a pool
like a deep ring.

What does it mean
when a middle-aged woman's
favorite dress is red?

When she looks out her window
and thinks of autumn leaves
as mounds of death?

Why is she going,
this woman who drives
to a cave,

throws down her purse
and pulls off her dress
like a flame?

His Leather Shoes Shone Like Jewels

(T. S. Eliot 1888-1965)

Acclaim ran shouting in
the Southern libraries;
the Midwest threw its
boundaries across the ocean
where you were only faintly
impressed, but happy to leave
business to bankers

who spoke the language
like English gentlemen.
What could have called you
back to a rough land
where men stood like
stacks of grain propped
up by insidious slogans?

In a boorish Texas town
where mud and sand mixed
in the oily evening,
your patine wit
popped up like pieces
of burnt toast.
Your words' fingers squeezed

the forms of dark articulation
into the red meat of meaning.
From the green fish's mouth
you chose a meter.
You placed your voice
on the rain when you came
before us. It held

firm as your stone craft.
Your furry cats and straw men
scratched and burned
at our leather shams.
And what can we say of your last words
but that all your erudition bent humbly
toward the ritual of Bethlehem.

Stripping the Bone

All the death drenched words
he wrings out like a red bandanna,
mopping the life from his face.
And places the long barrel
of morning on the last
day of his chest.
The wife will lie till the end,
reporting his slippers, his
undershirt ready for the expedition,
the horn glinting, the suit of lights
blowing its trumpets.
He stands at his desk,
bones breaking each other
for strength, the whiskey
waiting for evening,
when it's no longer needed.
Such a simple procedure
to pull the rag thru
the bore, look straight at
the silver rings spiraling
far as the eye can see,
farther than the ear chooses
to hear, down into
the father's cavern of shadows,
back into the simple pride
of the womb.

THIRTY YEARS IN A PIG STY

Reveille

(For Kirby Congdon)

Standing on my iron bed
my duty was
to unscrew the day,
to plunge us
into death, as night
burned out our eyes.

And when we lay
deep in the black river
floating on our dream
I alone held on
and woke us
to the memory
of the black sun.

The Hunter

Tonight I sit in my room
of a thousand eyes.

Somewhere a man looking
like a bear is writing me a letter.

(Shall I say there's a flea
in the oatmeal?)

He thinks of heavy apples
falling from the trees like fire.

The smell of burlap
covering his knees.

I crouch in a small room
counting the green flies.

Thirty Years in a Pig Sty

I eat, I sleep. For thirty
years I keep the slimy company
of pigs. This sty
they say is my prison. But
I escaped the Army's plague.
I saved my life
from governments.
By straining eyes I saw
the chinked world at work,
my eyes filled with tears.
From this solitary confinement
I've seen the world go by
and come again with daylight.
Oh yes, I missed my wife,
but handled it well enough
to know I was a man.
No jack boots trampled
on my ears.
The unpleasant dream of
waking from nightmare
into nightmare
was no more reality
than that of any man.
I was simply bored.
The common complaint
of those who have everything.

Confessions of an Inmate

My poems are affidavits
waiting to be signed
to commit me.

The fingers of each word
stitch straight jackets.

The cold hands build walls.

And I climb higher and higher
holding tight against the rungs of my shadow

till I see the barbed horizon
frowning beyond the forest of silent men.

SEEDTIME

At Rink's Club

Under the dark boards
of the dance floor that
hold the footprints,
the smell of our flesh
has fallen again.

The year the oak tree
wore galls. And you
with your woman-body, your face
already scarred like a storm.
I wasn't exactly disappointed
I didn't have you under the rocking
floor of the dance hall.

But now I must tell you,
stomping the truth
through these thin boards,
"I wish I could dance back
to the step I missed
for us both

and take you
on the hard ground.
And then I wouldn't keep
swaying, keep following you."

The Rattle

Is it their love of the dark
that makes us fear them?
Or a memory of an old tale
of gleeless dancers
jerking hideously, until
they broke their limbs?

Once I held a mouse by the
tail in an open field, and
once I dragged a dead rat
on a string as a plaything.

Shall I put on the face of
a cat to avoid any pity?
Is the rattle of a sack
a cause for alarm? What if
compassion's the shape
of an eye, the color
of a rat's stool?

The wedge of bread is laid
on the table, the edge of
the knife shimmers. Precisely
we slice it into squares,
then spread the silver paste,
sprinkle sugar into a sheen;
the brittle joke that will
choke their breath,
tarnish their pearl claws
before sunrise.

Flowing

The water comes flowing
into the sink. My face
runs down the drain
with shaving cream.
And still I see it
plainly in the mirror.

All truth is lies.

These blunt hairs
scraped from my jaw
thatch a roof in some village
under the sea. The blood
from this nick
trickles into ancient wineskins.

Think how many sinks are draining,
think of the flat rocks
where women are washing.

Cold Night

The bankers were dreaming of vaults,
the fire trucks asleep in their stalls
when the cold crept down thru the bones
of our hood and the carburetor died.
We'd thought to make it home
but the gauge was registering wrong.

Keep away Father & neighbors, we're drunk
on a Sailor's gin. Out of cigarettes,
an empty pack of fence posts,
an unwelcoming gravel drive.
The fawn lies in the upholstery
smooth as a young bride.
The armrest hangs out behind
like the paw of a lion.

> While someone's gone for
> gasoline we'll build
> a fire by the gate
> and wait, and wait, and
> wait.

Keep away Father & neighbors,

we're drunk on a Sailor's gin.

At home the mouse keeps
its place on the piano and
the bunny hides in the shade.
But now I'm drunk on
a Sailor's gin and morning
may bring disgrace.

Seedtime

We pushed down, past
the scars of our time

into the very hips
of suffering.

The land yawned like an iron clock
waiting for change.

There the weather
never said: I'm sorry.

We felt like old miners
sifting the grains.

The earth reached
down into rolling furrows.

Under the dirt, the seeds
began to sing.

What Can You Ask?

A broken face in the mirror.

A broken face in the mirror.

The peanut alone in the jar.

The boxcar desperate with peas.

The sunflower tiring of obligation.

The Lost Credit Card

So these are the things
we die for, we
live for.
The brick house
in the suburbs, the jacket
that doesn't fit, the fish scraping
its gills. All along
the moon remembered
its first tooth.
How can we make it up the steps
if the door at the bottom
isn't open?
The small wren building
its nest in the oven,
the rope twisted tight like
an almond.
The last leaf is opening
its tongue
on the horizon.
The fire goes
looking for its mate
in the ashes.
On the mountain
the owl is thrashing
a sermon.
The mad fox is
chasing the moon.

FIELD COMMAND

Black Train

All thru this corridor of night
the boxcars hold his passing.

The black train rolls frozen
on its rails, past the green

lights named "loner" and "sadskin."
Toward his nameless father

a man/child sleeps. Holding his
hands to his head, his is

the dream of forgetting,
the streets abandoned at

dawn. The mother is pushing
at numbers. School will not

meet this day for him. He
is gone, never to return

for supper. Layers of coats
are not enough to stop

the chill: the bright shirt
offers no fire or fuel.

And the black train rolls
on, never to return
to the station.

Stretching us Back into Time

TV cameras cast our sweating faces,
not the private tears we'd gushed
like a torrent of exploding glass
when angry stones leave vandal fingers.

No huge police dogs
snarled us in our place.
But noisy helicopter clatter,
municipal metronome, disturbed
our silent tribute
as we passed Lorraine:
where the cunning finger
had snatched Martin's life
from the cool April evening.

We marched through handbills
proclaiming martyrdom, through
lines of wrinkled uniforms
to marbled City Hall; where
platformed ministers and rotund
union leaders clapped and sang

with famous entertainers,
and white politicians in woolen suits
gave peace signs amid Black Power salutes,
"Tell it"'s and "A-men"'s

while our memories arched
like a threatened cat
stretching us back into time.

Field Command

Aged and florid, they go
arm in arm down lawns of corpses.
They rasp in fields of the young:
"The fault is not mine...not mine."

Elton Hayes: Murder by the
Memphis Police

The brain snows silence.
The first sign was the green ditch

rushing up the air, its engine
smelling like a copper casing.

The dull, quick thud in circles.
The scalded bark shining.

I have stolen a face from
the archives. In winter

the cement cracks like the
blow of a nightstick.

The sound of a white
hand clapping.

She Heat Her Bean

She grow they greens.
From cotton chop
suitcase she come.
From patch, she shelf and
she counter.
From stone she to hobble.

Thy sack and thy jar
she salt and she lard.
She scrub and she scar
are fish in thy dark.

In fat and in back
in hem on they floor
she stitch and she weave.
In fry and she bake
she bone are they juice.

In leg and they gizzard
she pick and she seed.
Thy ring and thy grill
in heat she her bean.
In grease she fly,
in fat she her nap.
She swipe in her skip,
she soy in she bus.

Pit and to iron
she tote and to steam.
In melon they soot
be cinder thy floor.

For wing she do draw
in ham hold her tongue.
Thy cake and thy stroke
she sweat and she bear.

She bleed in her black,
thy laugh in her fare.
In hold and in still
she heat her hot bean,
she sift her white meal.